CALIFORNIA DMV

EXAMS SUCCESS GUIDE WITH PAST
QUESTIONS AND ANSWERS

Kelvin Steve

Rights Reserved.

TABLE OF CONTENTS

INTRODUCTION

California, known for its diverse landscapes, bustling cities, and iconic highways, offers a unique driving experience like no other. Whether you're a seasoned driver looking to renew your license or a new driver eager to hit the road, it's imperative to be well-prepared to navigate California's roads safely. To help you on your journey, we present this comprehensive California Driving Test Question and Answer Guide.

This guide is designed to be your trusty companion, providing a wealth of essential information to ace your California driving test with confidence. From understanding the rules of the road to mastering the nuances of California-specific driving laws, we've got you covered. Our user-friendly format offers clear, concise explanations of the most important topics, along with a plethora of commonly asked questions and detailed answers to help you sharpen your knowledge and skills.

In the Golden State, responsible and safe driving is not just a necessity; it's a shared responsibility. By acquainting yourself with the material within these pages, you'll be better equipped to make informed, safe decisions while driving on California's highways, freeways, and city streets. Whether you're preparing for the written exam, the behind-the-wheel test, or simply seeking a refresher, our guide aims to make your journey to becoming a licensed California driver as smooth as the pavement you'll traverse.

So, fasten your seatbelt, adjust your mirrors, and get ready to embark on a learning journey that will not only help you pass your California driving test but also equip you to become a responsible, confident, and safe driver in this remarkable state. Let's start this engine of knowledge and explore the answers to the questions you need to succeed on your California driving test.

Driving Rules, Signals, Markings, and Road Signs

Have you ever passed a road sign and realized you didn't understand what the message or symbol was telling you to do? Or have you ever wondered if the color and shape of the road sign have a specific meaning? Or simply curious about the meaning of the road sign?

Drivers must be able to identify road sign meanings quickly and accurately. Understanding must also take place while traveling at what may be high speeds. For that and other reasons, a universal set of guidelines has been established to help people quickly answer, "what do road signs mean?" while driving.

With so many signs on the road, it's easy to get confused wondering about road signs and meanings. The problem is compounded when language barriers, color vision deficiencies, and illiteracy are factored into the equation. Unfortunately, one wrong interpretation of road sign meanings can lead to a serious accident or injury.

To help prevent this, the U.S. Department of Transportation (DOT) has increasingly used symbols rather than words to convey the different safety messages on roadways and highways. Pictograms and symbols are easier to recognize and understand, cross various language barriers, and often close the communication gap. Symbols are quickly becoming the standard for traffic control devices throughout the world.

Understanding the traffic signs and meanings can be as simple as recognizing what the colors, shapes, and symbols on the sign represent. For many drivers, this system eliminates the need to read road signs and allows for quick identification of the intended meaning.

For instance, the colors that make up all road signs are an essential indicator of the information they contain. The standards for the design and application of the signs as controlled under the Manual on Uniform Traffic Control Devices (MUTCD) explain the significance of the colors on road traffic signs.

Road Sign Color Meanings
1. Red: Red generally means stop. The use of red on signs is limited to stop, yield, and prohibition signs.
White: A white background indicates a regulatory sign.
Yellow: Yellow conveys a general caution message.
Green: Green shows permitted traffic movements or directional guidance.
2. Fluorescent yellow/green: Indicates pedestrian crossings and school zones.
3. Orange: Orange is used for warning and guidance in roadway work zones.

4. Coral: Coral is used for incident management signs.

Blue: Blue indicates road user services, tourist information, and evacuation routes.

Brown: Brown is used to showing guidance to sites of public recreation or cultural interest.

Although the colors play a critical factor in providing consistency throughout the roads and highways, each shape of road signs has a specific meaning, as well. The shape of road traffic signs can alert drivers about the message prior to reading the contents. Depending on weather conditions, the only thing you might be able to make out is the shape of the sign. If that's the case – the shape of the sign is just as critical as the message, if not more.

Road Sign Shape Meanings

Many road sign meanings can also be established through their outlines. For drivers unable to determine a sign's color, the shape could play a pivotal role in conveying the intent or meaning of road signs.

An octagon road sign conveys the need to stop. A stop sign is the only sign that uses this shape. Combined with its red background, the unique shape makes it easily recognizable even at great distances.

An upside-down triangle road sign always means "yield."

Diamond-shaped road signs always warn of possible hazards ahead. These are traffic signs, temporary traffic control signs, and some pedestrian and bicycle signs.
Pennant-shaped road signs warn drivers of no-passing zones.

Round-shaped road signs are used for railroad signs. When you see a round traffic sign, you will likely see a railroad crossing or light rail transit crossing signs ahead. A pentagon-shaped road sign provides a warning that a school zone is ahead or a school crossing zone is approaching.

A square or horizontal rectangle-shaped road sign usually provides guidance to drivers but can be used for a variety of needs. Some common uses for this shape include exit closed, detour, and parking indicator road signs.

Vertical rectangle road signs are typically used to inform drivers of regulatory notices, such as speed limits.
There are some exceptions to the shape and color rules for road sign meanings. For example, the railroad crossbuck sign is an indicator of an upcoming railroad crossing, but it is not circular. However, the generally uniform application of standards makes it easy to ascertain the meaning of road signs when driving.

The MUTCD has specific requirements for the size of signs and the material the message is printed on, in addition to the color, shape, and symbol as mentioned above. For example, when signs are used at night, they need to be either retroreflective, with a material that has a smooth, sealed outer surface, or illuminated to show similar shape and color both day and night. However, custom traffic signs are often needed for unique messages, too.

Now that you know the answer to "what do road signs mean?" when it comes to colors and shapes, take a few minutes to read what road sign symbols mean and see a few examples

Defensive Driving and Safety Measures

To reduce the risk of accidents and maintain safe driving, it's important to adopt a defensive driving approach. If you've spent any time on the road, you're likely aware that not all drivers exhibit good driving habits, even though many believe they do. Some drivers drive aggressively, while others may drift into other lanes due to distractions. Tailgating, sudden, un-signaled turns, and weaving through traffic are also common issues.

Aggressive drivers are a significant cause of road accidents, accounting for approximately one-third of all traffic crashes. However, the problem of inattentive or distracted driving is on the rise, as people attempt to multitask by talking on the phone, texting, eating, or even watching TV while driving.

While you can't control the behavior of other drivers, you can enhance your own safety by improving your defensive driving skills.

Here are some skills that empower you to stay in control behind the wheel:

1. Maintain focus: Driving is primarily a mental task, requiring constant attention to factors such as road conditions, speed, adherence to traffic laws, signs, signals, and the actions of other vehicles. Staying focused solely on driving is essential for safe navigation. Distractions, such as phone calls or eating, can impede your ability to identify potential issues and respond appropriately. It's not just inexperienced drivers; even those with years of driving experience can become complacent. All drivers should remind themselves to remain attentive.

2. Stay alert: Being alert, free from drowsiness or the influence of substances, allows you to respond swiftly to unexpected situations, like a car suddenly braking in front of you. Alcohol, drugs (including both prescription and over-the-counter medications), and drowsiness all affect a driver's reaction time and decision-making. Fatigue is a leading contributor to accidents, so ensure you are well-rested before embarking on a road trip."

"Stay vigilant for other drivers and road users. Part of maintaining control on the road involves being aware of the actions of those around you and anticipating their potential maneuvers to avoid being caught off guard. For instance, if a car speeds past you on the highway with limited space between it and a slow-moving truck in the same lane, it's highly likely that the driver will attempt to merge into your lane just in front of you. Anticipating the actions of other drivers and making necessary adjustments is a key strategy for reducing your risk.

When practicing defensive driving, you remain alert and prepared for any unforeseen circumstances. You exercise caution but are ready to take action rather than relying on the behavior of other drivers. According to the U.S. Department of Transportation, 90% of accidents are attributed to driver errors.

Following these defensive driving guidelines can help mitigate your risks while on the road:
1. Prioritize safety. Avoid exhibiting aggressive or inattentive driving behavior, as this positions you better to deal with the poor driving habits of others. Maintain a safe following distance between your vehicle and the one in front. Always secure your doors and wear your seatbelt to safeguard against ejection in the event of a collision.
2. Stay aware of your surroundings and pay close attention. Frequently check your mirrors and assess conditions 20 to 30 seconds ahead of your current position. Keep your eyes in motion. If you notice signs of aggressive driving from another vehicle, reduce your speed or pull over to avoid potential dangers. If you're concerned about another driver's reckless behavior, consider getting off the road by turning right or taking

the next exit if it's safe. Additionally, be vigilant for pedestrians, cyclists, and animals along the roadway.

3. Avoid relying on the actions of other drivers. While being considerate, always look out for your own safety. Don't assume that another driver will yield or allow you to merge. Instead, anticipate that drivers may disregard red lights or stop signs, and be prepared to respond. Plan your maneuvers with the worst-case scenario in mind.

4. Adhere to the 3- to 4-second rule. Given that the highest risk of collision is in front of your vehicle, following the 3- to 4-second rule helps you maintain a safe following distance and provides adequate braking time if needed. However, this rule applies to normal traffic under good weather conditions. In adverse conditions like rain, fog, night driving, or when following a large vehicle or motorcycle, increase your following distance by an additional second for each condition.

5. Control your speed. Posted speed limits are applicable under ideal conditions. It's your responsibility to adjust your speed according to the current road and weather conditions. Higher speeds make it more challenging to control your vehicle in case of unexpected events. Managing your speed is crucial for maintaining control.

6. Always have an escape route. To avoid potential hazards, position your vehicle where you have the best visibility and can be seen by others. Having an alternate path of travel is essential, so ensure there's a way to

maneuver your vehicle if your immediate route is suddenly blocked.

7. Address risks separately. When confronted with multiple risks, it's best to address them one at a time. The goal is to avoid dealing with too many risks simultaneously.

8. Eliminate distractions. Any activity that diverts your attention from driving is a distraction. Driving deserves your full focus, so remain committed to the task at hand.

The Best Strategies to Pass the Exam Free from Anxiety and Doubt

Facing an exam, particularly one as significant as the DMV test, can often trigger feelings of anxiety and doubt. This section of the resource, "The Best Strategies to Pass Exam Free from Anxiety and Doubt," is dedicated to addressing these concerns and providing actionable techniques to help you approach your DMV exam with confidence.

Understanding Exam Anxiety

Exam anxiety, also known as test anxiety, is a common psychological response that many individuals experience when faced with the prospect of an upcoming exam. It's essential to delve into this phenomenon and understand its nature before embarking on the journey to conquer it effectively. This section aims to provide a comprehensive insight into what exam anxiety is and why it occurs:

1. The Nature of Exam Anxiety: Exam anxiety is a normal emotional reaction that arises when we perceive a threat or challenge in the form of an exam. It's characterized by a range of physical, emotional, and cognitive symptoms, including increased heart rate, sweaty palms, nervousness, self-doubt, and racing thoughts. These reactions can be distressing and interfere with your ability to perform at your best.

2. Common Triggers: This segment delves into the common triggers of exam anxiety, which often include the fear of failure, the pressure to succeed, and the uncertainty of the outcome. Understanding these triggers helps you identify the specific areas you need to address.

3.Recognizing You're Not Alone: Exam anxiety is a widespread experience. It's reassuring to know that you're not alone in dealing with this challenge. Many individuals, even high-achievers, grapple with anxiety before exams. Recognizing this fact can help ease the sense of isolation or inadequacy that sometimes accompanies anxiety.

4.The Impact on Performance: It's important to realize that exam anxiety can significantly impact your performance. It may lead to blanking out, difficulty concentrating, and decreased recall of important information. This section highlights how unchecked anxiety can hinder your ability to showcase your true knowledge.

5.Managing Exam Anxiety as a Skill: Examining anxiety is not merely a problem to overcome but a skill to master. By understanding its nature and triggers, you gain the power to manage and even reduce its impact. This section empowers you by framing exam anxiety as a challenge that can be effectively addressed.

The Importance of Preparation: Effective preparation plays a pivotal role in managing anxiety. Understanding the material thoroughly and being well-acquainted with the exam format can bolster your confidence and reduce anxiety. This introduction paves the way for the subsequent strategies, emphasizing that knowledge and practice are your allies in the battle against exam anxiety

Strategy 1: Preparation and Practice

In the realm of exam success, preparation and practice are your trusty allies. This strategy is the first crucial step towards conquering DMV exam anxiety, ensuring that you're equipped with the knowledge and confidence to perform at your best. Here's a more in-depth exploration of this key strategy:

1.Getting to Know the Exam Format: One of the initial actions is understanding the format of the DMV exam. The DMV typically administers written exams that cover various aspects of driving rules, regulations, road signs, and safe driving practices. Knowing the format and structure of the test helps in directing your preparation efforts effectively.

2. Reviewing Essential Materials: This strategy involves diving into the essential study materials that pertain to the DMV exam. These materials may include the driver's manual, online resources, and any specific study guides. This thorough review helps you grasp the critical information needed to pass the exam.

3.Practice, Practice, Practice: Practicing with sample questions is a cornerstone of this strategy. It's akin to a dress rehearsal for the big performance. This section may include tips on finding practice exams online or utilizing practice questions provided within the resource. By repeatedly answering these questions, you become more comfortable with the exam's content and format.

4. Identifying Knowledge Gaps: The process of practice often reveals areas where you may be less confident. This is a valuable discovery, as it directs your focus towards specific topics that require further attention. Addressing these knowledge gaps is a key aspect of thorough preparation.

5. Building Confidence: As you progress through your preparation and practice, you're building a sense of confidence. The more you familiarize yourself with the material and the format of the exam, the less daunting it becomes. This newfound confidence is a potent antidote to exam anxiety.

6. Creating a Study Schedule: Effective time management is an integral part of this strategy. The creation of a study schedule allows you to allocate time for review, practice, and self-assessment. A well-structured schedule ensures that you cover all necessary material without feeling rushed or overwhelmed.

7. Mock Exams: In addition to sample questions, this section may introduce the concept of mock exams. Mock exams simulate the actual DMV exam experience, complete with time constraints. Taking these mock exams under test-like conditions further boosts your readiness and enhances your ability to manage anxiety during the real exam.

8. Progress Tracking: As you progress through your preparation and practice, tracking your improvement can be a source of motivation. This section may suggest keeping a log of your performance on practice exams, highlighting areas of improvement, and celebrating your progress.

The "Preparation and Practice" strategy is not only about absorbing information but also about building confidence and resilience. It ensures that you are well-prepared to tackle the DMV exam head-on, armed with knowledge and experience. This strategy, when executed diligently, is a significant step towards minimizing anxiety and maximizing your chances of success.

Strategy 2: Stress Management Techniques

The second strategy, "Stress Management Techniques," plays a pivotal role in helping you navigate the waters of DMV exam preparation with a calm and focused mindset. Stress and anxiety can be formidable adversaries when preparing for a high-stakes examination, but they can be effectively managed with the right techniques. Here's a more detailed exploration of this crucial strategy:

1. Understanding Stress and Anxiety: This segment delves into the concepts of stress and anxiety, explaining how they manifest both physically and mentally. It's important to recognize the signs of stress and anxiety in order to address them effectively.

2. Deep Breathing and Relaxation Exercises: One of the foundational techniques for managing stress is deep breathing. This strategy may introduce the concept of diaphragmatic breathing, where you focus on slow, deep breaths to calm your nervous system. Relaxation exercises, such as progressive muscle relaxation, can also be discussed.

3.Mindfulness and Meditation: Practicing mindfulness involves being fully present in the moment and can help alleviate anxiety. Meditation techniques, even short sessions, can assist in reducing stress and promoting mental clarity.

4. Positive Self-talk: This section emphasizes the power of positive self-talk. It encourages you to replace self-doubt and negative thoughts with affirmations and encouraging statements. Building a positive inner dialogue is a key aspect of managing anxiety.

5. Time Management: Effective time management techniques can significantly reduce stress. This strategy may introduce tips for creating a study schedule that optimizes your time, minimizes last-minute cramming, and ensures a balanced approach to preparation.

6. Exercise and Physical Activity: Physical activity is a proven method for reducing stress and anxiety. This section might discuss the benefits of incorporating regular exercise into your routine, even if it's just a brief daily walk.

7. Nutrition and Hydration: What you eat and drink can have a significant impact on your stress levels. This strategy may touch on the importance of a balanced diet and staying adequately hydrated to support your mental and physical well-being.

8. Sleep Quality: A good night's sleep is vital for stress management and cognitive function. This section could explore tips for improving sleep quality, including maintaining a consistent sleep schedule and creating a relaxing bedtime routine.

9.Seeking Support: Stress management doesn't have to be a solo endeavor. This segment may suggest reaching out to friends, family, or a mentor for emotional support and guidance when dealing with anxiety.

10. Realistic Goal-setting: Setting achievable goals for your exam preparation is essential. This strategy encourages you to set realistic expectations and not overwhelm yourself with unattainable objectives.

By adopting these stress management techniques, you gain the tools to maintain a balanced, focused, and anxiety-free approach to your DMV exam preparation. This strategy isn't just about mitigating stress temporarily but fostering a lifestyle that promotes overall well-being and success. It complements your knowledge preparation by ensuring that your mindset is equally well-prepared for the challenges of the exam.

Strategy 3: Positive Mindset and Visualization

One of the most powerful tools for conquering DMV exam anxiety is the ability to cultivate a positive mindset. This third strategy, "Positive Mindset and Visualization," focuses on harnessing the strength of your thoughts and mental imagery to instill confidence and reduce doubt. Let's delve deeper into this empowering strategy:

1. Recognizing and Redirecting Negative Thoughts: Examining the sources of negative thoughts and self-doubt is essential. This part may include exercises and techniques for recognizing these thoughts and redirecting them towards more constructive and positive self-talk.

2. Affirmations and Positive Declarations: This strategy encourages you to develop a repertoire of affirmations and positive declarations. These are short, powerful statements that reaffirm your abilities and instill confidence. Repeating these affirmations regularly can help rewire your thought patterns.

3. Visualization Techniques: Visualization is a key component of this strategy. It involves mentally rehearsing your success. This section may guide you through the process of visualizing yourself taking the DMV exam, answering questions with ease, and ultimately passing the test. Visualization creates a mental image of success, which can be a potent motivator and confidence booster.

4. Setting Clear Goals: Setting clear and achievable goals is essential. This section emphasizes the importance of establishing specific objectives for your DMV exam, as well as for your preparation. These goals act as guiding stars, helping you stay on track and maintaining a positive mindset.

5. Handling Setbacks: Preparing for an exam doesn't always go smoothly, and setbacks can happen. This part may offer advice on how to handle setbacks and disappointments with a positive mindset. It encourages you to view challenges as opportunities for growth rather than as failures.

6. Staying in the Present: Dwelling on past mistakes or worrying about future outcomes can lead to anxiety. This strategy introduces the concept of staying in the present moment and focusing on the tasks at hand, rather than getting caught up in anxiety-inducing thoughts about the future.

DMV PAST QUESTIONS AND ANSWERS

1. Question: What does a single solid white line across an intersection mean?
Answer: It means you must stop behind the line for a traffic signal or sign.

2. Question: When should you use your horn?
Answer: To alert others of your presence if you think they might not see you.

3. Question: What should you do if you're approaching a railroad crossing with lowered gates and flashing lights?
Answer: Stop and wait until the gates are raised and the lights stop flashing.

4. Question: What's the maximum speed limit in California for a school zone when children are present?
Answer: 25 mph.

5. Question: If you're under 21, what is the minimum BAC (blood alcohol content) level for being arrested for DUI?
Answer: 0.01%.

6. Question: What's the basic speed law in California?
Answer: Do not drive at a speed greater than is reasonable and prudent.

7. Question: How far in advance should you signal your intention to turn?
Answer: At least 100 feet before the turn.

8. Question: When can you legally make a U-turn in a residential area?
Answer: When it's safe, and there are no vehicles approaching.

9. Question: What should you do if you're approaching a roundabout?
Answer: Slow down and yield to vehicles already in the roundabout.

10. Question: What's the penalty for littering on a California highway?
Answer: A fine of up to $1,000 and community service.

11. Question: When is it legal to pass on the right?
Answer: When the vehicle ahead is making a left turn and there is a lane available for passing.

12. Question: What's the maximum speed limit for a truck or bus on certain California highways?

Answer: 55 mph.

13. Question: What should you do if your vehicle starts to hydroplane?
Answer: Ease off the gas, do not brake, and steer in the direction you want to go.

14. Question: When should you use your headlights?
Answer: Between sunset and sunrise and when visibility is less than 1,000 feet.

15. Question: What's the minimum age to apply for a provisional driver's license in California?
Answer: 16 years old.

16. Question: How far must you park from a fire hydrant?
Answer: 15 feet.

17. Question: What should you do if you see a pedestrian with a white cane at a crosswalk?
Answer: Stop and yield the right-of-way.

18. Question: When can you pass a school bus that has stopped with its red lights flashing?
Answer: Never, unless you're on the opposite side of a divided highway.

19. Question: What's the legal maximum blood alcohol concentration (BAC) for drivers 21 and over?
Answer: 0.08%.

20. Question: What should you do if you're involved in a collision and no one is injured but there's property damage over $1,000?
Answer: File a Report of Traffic Accident with the DMV.

21. Question: When should you use your headlights during inclement weather?
Answer: Anytime visibility is less than 1,000 feet.

22. Question: What's the penalty for a first-time DUI conviction in California?
Answer: A fine, license suspension, and possible imprisonment.

23. Question: When are you allowed to use your horn in a residential area?
Answer: Only in an emergency.

24. Question: What's the maximum speed limit for a school bus when carrying children?
Answer: 45 mph.

25. Question: How far should you stop from a railroad crossing when there is a stop sign?
Answer: No closer than 15 feet.

26. Question: What's the "right of way"?
Answer: The privilege of having immediate use of a certain part of a roadway.

27. Question: What's the purpose of a crosswalk sign?
Answer: To alert drivers to the presence of a crosswalk.

28. Question: What's the penalty for failing to stop for a school bus with flashing red lights?
Answer: A fine and possible license suspension.

29. Question: How close can you legally park to a driveway entrance?
Answer: No closer than 3 feet.

30. Question: What's the maximum speed limit for a passenger vehicle on most California highways?
Answer: 65 mph.

31. Question: What should you do if you're approaching a blind intersection?
Answer: Slow down and be prepared for a stop if necessary.

32. Question: What's the penalty for driving under the influence of alcohol or drugs?
Answer: Fines, license suspension, and possible imprisonment.

33. Question: What should you do if you're driving and you see a green traffic sign?
Answer: Follow the direction on the sign.

34. Question: When are you allowed to make a U-turn in a business district?
Answer: When there is no vehicle within 200 feet approaching.

35. Question: What's the purpose of a white diamond on the road?
Answer: It marks carpool lanes.

36. Question: When is it legal to park on a freeway?
Answer: Only in an emergency.

37. Question: What's the "three-second rule" for following other vehicles?
Answer: Maintain a following distance that would take at least three seconds to reach the same point as the vehicle ahead.

38. Question: What should you do if your vehicle's accelerator pedal sticks?
Answer: Shift to neutral and apply the brakes.

39. Question: What should you do when passing a bicycle?
Answer: Allow a minimum of 3 feet of clearance between your vehicle and the bicycle.

40. Question: What's the maximum speed limit for a passenger vehicle on two-lane undivided highways?
Answer: 55 mph.

41. Question: What should you do if you miss your exit on the freeway?
Answer: Continue to the next exit.

42. Question: What should you do if you're involved in a collision where someone is injured, but you're not at fault?

Answer: Give your information to the injured person, but do not admit fault.

43. Question: When must you yield the right-of-way to emergency vehicles using sirens and lights?
Answer: Immediately, and move to the right edge of the road.

44. Question: When should you use your high-beam headlights?
Answer: In rural areas when there are no oncoming vehicles.

45. Question: What's the purpose of a yellow and black circular sign?
Answer: It indicates a railroad crossing ahead.

46. Question: When is it legal to pass a vehicle on the right?
Answer: When the vehicle ahead is making or about to make a left turn.

47. Question: What should you do when an emergency vehicle with its lights flashing approaches while you're in an intersection?
Answer: Continue through the intersection and then pull over to the right.

48. Question: When should you use your turn signals?
Answer: At least 100 feet before turning.

49. Question: What's the maximum speed limit for a vehicle towing another vehicle?
Answer: 55 mph.

50. Question: What's the penalty for not stopping for a school bus with flashing red lights on a two-lane road?
Answer: A fine and possible license suspension.

51. Question: When are you allowed to drive on the shoulder of a road?
Answer: Only to pass another vehicle.

52. Question: What's the minimum following distance when driving behind a motorcycle?
Answer: A minimum of three seconds.

53. Question: What should you do if you encounter a large vehicle on a narrow road?
Answer: Slow down and let the large vehicle pass.

54. Question: What's the maximum speed limit for a passenger vehicle when towing another vehicle on a two-lane undivided highway?
Answer: 55 mph.

55. Question: When must you always stop at a railroad crossing?
Answer: When a train is approaching and the crossing signals are flashing.

56. Question: What should you do if you have a tire blowout?

Answer: Grip the steering wheel firmly and ease off the gas.

57. Question: When are you allowed to use your cellphone while driving in California?
Answer: Only with a hands-free device.

58. Question: What's the purpose of a red octagonal sign?
Answer: It's a stop sign, meaning you must come to a complete stop.

59. Question: What's the purpose of a red and white triangular sign?
Answer: It's a yield sign, indicating you must slow down and be prepared to stop if necessary.

60. Question: What's the speed limit in a business district?
Answer: 25 mph.

61. Question: What's the legal minimum age for passengers in the front seat of a vehicle with an active airbag?
Answer: 12 years old.

62. Question: What should you do if you're driving and encounter a school bus with flashing amber lights?
Answer: Slow down and prepare to stop.

63. Question: What should you do if you're approaching an intersection where the traffic lights are not working?
Answer: Treat it as a four-way stop.

64. Question: When can you legally drive in a bike lane?
Answer: Never, unless you're within 200 feet of an intersection preparing to make a turn.

65. Question: What should you do if your brakes suddenly fail?
Answer: Pump the brake pedal, use the parking brake, and downshift to a lower gear.

66. Question: When must you dim your headlights to low beam when following another vehicle?
Answer: Within 300 feet when driving behind another vehicle.

67. Question: What's the maximum speed limit on most two-lane highways in California?
Answer: 55 mph.

68. Question: What should you do when making a left turn at an intersection?

Answer: Yield to oncoming traffic and pedestrians.

69. Question: When can you make a U-turn in a residential area?
Answer: When safe and legal, such as at an intersection.

70. Question: What's the maximum speed limit on a California highway for trucks and vehicles towing trailers?
Answer: 55 mph.

71. Question: When is it safe to return to the lane after passing another vehicle?
Answer: When you can see the entire front of the vehicle you passed in your rearview mirror.

72. Question: What should you do when approaching a stopped emergency vehicle with its lights flashing on the opposite side of a divided highway?
Answer: Slow down and proceed with caution.

73. Question: When should you yield the right-of-way at an uncontrolled T-intersection?
Answer: To the vehicle on the through road.

74. Question: What should you do if you're involved in a collision with an unattended vehicle?

Answer: Leave a note with your contact information and report it to the police.

75. Question: What's the maximum speed limit in a residential area?
Answer: 25 mph.

76. Question: When should you use tire chains on your vehicle?
Answer: When required by Caltrans due to snow or icy conditions.

77. Question: What's the purpose of a green and white rectangular sign?
Answer: It provides information and guidance.

78. Question: What should you do if you see a pedestrian with a white cane at an intersection?
Answer: Stop and yield the right-of-way.

79. Question: What should you do when approaching a school bus with flashing red lights on a divided highway?
Answer: You may continue driving, but be cautious.

80. Question: When should you use your hazard lights?
Answer: Only when your vehicle is stopped or disabled on the roadway.

81. Question: What should you do if you're approaching an intersection and the traffic signal changes from green to yellow?
Answer: Slow down and prepare to stop if you can do so safely.

82. Question: What's the legal maximum speed limit in a school zone when children are present?
Answer: 25 mph.

83. Question: What should you do if you're pulled over by a law enforcement officer?
Answer: Pull to the right as far as possible, turn off your engine, and stay in the vehicle.

84. Question: When should you yield the right-of-way to pedestrians in a crosswalk?
Answer: Always, even if the crosswalk is not marked.

85. Question: What should you do if you miss your exit on the freeway and there's no other exit nearby?
Answer: Continue to the next exit.

86. Question: When should you use your parking lights?
Answer: Never use parking lights while driving.

87. Question: What should you do when approaching a blind intersection with no stop signs or signals?
Answer: Slow down and be prepared for a stop if necessary.

88. Question: When must you stop for a school bus with flashing red lights on a two-lane road?
Answer: In both directions, unless there's a divided highway or physical barrier.

89. Question: When should you use your high-beam headlights?
Answer: In rural areas when there are no oncoming vehicles or when driving on dark roads.

90. Question: What should you do if you're stopped at a red traffic signal and it turns green?
Answer: Check for traffic and proceed when it's safe.

91. Question: What's the maximum speed limit for a vehicle with three or more axles on most California highways?
Answer: 55 mph.

92. Question: When are you allowed to drive on the shoulder to pass another vehicle?
Answer: Never, unless it's a legal designated lane.

93. Question: What should you do if you're involved in a collision and there are no injuries but there's property damage over $750?
Answer: Report the collision to the DMV.

94. Question: What's the penalty for failing to stop at a stop sign?
Answer: Fines and possible points on your driving record.

95. Question: When should you use your low-beam headlights?
Answer: In fog, heavy rain, or snowy conditions.

96. Question: What should you do when merging onto a freeway?
Answer: Accelerate to the speed of freeway traffic before merging.

97. Question: What's the maximum speed limit for vehicles with two or three axles on most California highways?
Answer: 65 mph.

98. Question: What should you do when approaching a flashing red traffic signal?
Answer: Come to a complete stop and proceed when safe.

99. Question: When must you always stop for a school bus?
Answer: When it's loading or unloading children.

100. Question: What's the maximum speed limit in a residential area near a senior center, school, or hospital?
Answer: 25 mph.

101. Question: What should you do when entering a curve?
Answer: Slow down before entering the curve.

102. Question: What should you do when driving in foggy conditions?
Answer: Use low-beam headlights and reduce your speed.

103. Question: What should you do if you're involved in a collision and someone is injured?
Answer: Render aid and notify law enforcement.

104. Question: What should you do if you're involved in a collision with a parked vehicle and can't find the owner?
Answer: Leave a note with your contact information on the parked vehicle.

105. Question: What should you do if you encounter a slow-moving vehicle on a two-lane road?
Answer: Wait for a safe opportunity to pass when it's legal.

106. Question: When are you allowed to pass on the right?
Answer: When the vehicle ahead is making or about to make a left turn.

107. Question: What should you do if you're driving and an animal crosses your path?
Answer: Slow down and try to stop or safely avoid the animal.

108. Question: When can you use your vehicle's horn?
Answer: To alert others of your presence when necessary for safety.

109. Question: What's the maximum speed limit for vehicles towing trailers or campers?
Answer: 55 mph.

110. Question: What should you do when approaching a stopped emergency vehicle with its lights flashing on a two-lane road?
Answer: Slow down and move to the lane farthest from the emergency vehicle if safe.

111. Question: What should you do when approaching a roundabout?
Answer: Slow down and yield to traffic in the roundabout.

112. Question: What should you do when approaching a stopped school bus with flashing red lights on a multi-lane road?
Answer: Stop, regardless of the number of lanes.

113. Question: What should you do when you see a pedestrian using a white cane at a crosswalk?
Answer: Stop and allow the pedestrian to cross.

114. Question: What should you do when you see a yellow and black circular sign?
Answer: Prepare to stop, such as for a railroad crossing.

115. Question: When should you use your parking brake?
Answer: Whenever you park your vehicle.

116. Question: When are you allowed to pass another vehicle on the right?
Answer: On multi-lane highways with two or more lanes traveling in the same direction.

117. Question: What's the maximum speed limit on most California highways for vehicles towing trailers or campers?
Answer: 55 mph.

118. Question: What should you do if you're involved in a collision with another vehicle?
Answer: Exchange information with the other driver and report it to law enforcement.

119. Question: What should you do when approaching a flashing yellow traffic signal?
Answer: Slow down and proceed with caution.

120. Question: What's the maximum speed limit for vehicles under 3,000 pounds on most California highways?
Answer: 70 mph.

121. Question: What should you do when you're on a freeway and want to exit?
Answer: Signal and move into the exit lane well before reaching the exit.

122. Question: When must you stop for a school bus with flashing red lights on a divided highway?
Answer: Only if you're traveling on the same side of the road as the school bus.

123. Question: What should you do if your vehicle's wheels drift onto the shoulder of the road?
Answer: Gradually release the gas pedal and steer back onto the roadway.

124. Question: When are you allowed to pass on the left?
Answer: When the vehicle ahead is making or about to make a left turn.

125. Question: What should you do if you're involved in a collision where there are no injuries and property damage is less than $750?
Answer: Exchange information with the other driver and report the collision to the DMV.

126. Question: When should you use your headlights?
Answer: Half an hour after sunset and half an hour before sunrise.

127. Question: What should you do if a vehicle's lights aren't on during rain or fog?
Answer: Turn on your own headlights and increase following distance.

128. Question: When must you yield the right-of-way to other vehicles?
Answer: When it is necessary for safety.

129. Question: What should you do when you're driving on the freeway and a large truck is passing you?
Answer: Stay to the right and slow down to make it easier for the truck to pass.

130. Question: What should you do if you're driving on the freeway and miss your exit?
Answer: Continue to the next exit and turn around.

131. Question: What should you do when approaching a blind intersection with a stop sign?
Answer: Come to a complete stop and proceed when it's safe.

132. Question: When are you allowed to make a U-turn at a traffic signal?
Answer: Unless prohibited, when the way is clear.

133. Question: What should you do when approaching a school zone with children present?
Answer: Slow down and be prepared to stop.

134. Question: What should you do if you're involved in a collision and someone is injured but can't communicate?
Answer: Render aid if possible and notify law enforcement.

135. Question: What should you do when you approach an intersection with a stop sign and a crosswalk but no stop line?
Answer: Stop before the crosswalk.

136. Question: When must you yield the right-of-way to pedestrians using a crosswalk?
Answer: Always, even if the crosswalk is not marked.

137. Question: What should you do when entering a freeway?
Answer: Accelerate to the speed of freeway traffic before merging.

138. Question: What should you do if you're involved in a collision and your vehicle is blocking traffic?
Answer: Move your vehicle out of the traffic lane if possible.

139. Question: When can you make a legal U-turn in a residential area?
Answer: When safe, and there are no vehicles approaching within 200 feet.

140. Question: What should you do when approaching an intersection with a flashing yellow signal?
Answer: Slow down and proceed with caution.

141. Question: What should you do when approaching an intersection with a steady yellow traffic signal?
Answer: Slow down and prepare to stop, as the signal is about to turn red.

142. Question: What should you do when a school bus is stopped on a two-lane road with its flashing red lights on?
Answer: Stop in both directions, regardless of your direction of travel.

143. Question: What should you do when merging onto a freeway?
Answer: Accelerate to the speed of freeway traffic before merging.

144. Question: What should you do when driving on a road with two or more lanes in the same direction?
Answer: Stay in the right lane except to pass slower vehicles.

145. Question: When are you allowed to cross a solid yellow line on your side of the road?
Answer: To make a left turn into or from an alley, private road, or driveway.

146. Question: What should you do when a pedestrian is in a crosswalk with flashing or steady "DON'T WALK" signals?
Answer: Yield the right-of-way and do not enter the crosswalk.

147. Question: What should you do when approaching a roundabout?
Answer: Slow down and yield to traffic in the roundabout.

148. Question: What should you do when driving on a freeway with multiple lanes?
Answer: Keep right except to pass slower vehicles.

149. Question: What should you do when driving behind a large truck or bus?
Answer: Stay out of their "no-zones" or blind spots.

150. Question: When can you legally use a cell phone without a hands-free device while driving?
Answer: Only to make emergency calls to law enforcement or other emergency services.

151. Question: What should you do when driving in adverse weather conditions, such as rain or snow?
Answer: Slow down and increase following distance.

152. Question: What should you do when approaching a pedestrian with a guide dog or white cane at a crosswalk?
Answer: Stop and yield the right-of-way.

153. Question: What should you do when you see a "lane use control" signal?
Answer: Obey the signal, which indicates which lanes can be used at that time.

154. Question: What should you do when driving near a blind pedestrian who is carrying a white cane or using a guide dog?
Answer: Slow down and be prepared to stop.

155. Question: What should you do when you encounter a funeral procession with lights and sirens?
Answer: Pull over to the right and stop, as you would for any emergency vehicle.

156. Question: What should you do when you see a "Yield" sign?
Answer: Slow down or stop if necessary and yield the right-of-way to other traffic.

157. Question: What should you do when driving near a school with children present?

Answer: Slow down and watch for children walking or playing near the road.

158. Question: What should you do when you see a "No Turn on Red" sign?
Answer: Do not make a right turn on a red traffic signal at that intersection.

159. Question: What should you do when you see a "No Parking" sign?
Answer: Do not park in the area indicated by the sign.

160. Question: What should you do when you see a "Do Not Enter" sign?
Answer: Do not enter the road or freeway in the direction shown on the sign.

161. Question: What should you do when you encounter a "One Way" sign?
Answer: Drive only in the direction indicated by the sign.

162. Question: What should you do when you see a "No U-Turn" sign?
Answer: Do not make a U-turn at that location.

163. Question: What should you do when you see a "No Right Turn" sign?

Answer: Do not make a right turn at that location.

164. Question: What should you do when you see a "No Left Turn" sign?
Answer: Do not make a left turn at that location.

165. Question: What should you do when you see a "No Stopping" sign?
Answer: Do not stop your vehicle in the area indicated by the sign.

166. Question: What should you do when you see a "Wrong Way" sign?
Answer: Do not enter the road or freeway in the direction shown on the sign.

167. Question: What should you do when you encounter a "Railroad Crossing" sign?
Answer: Slow down and be prepared to stop if you see or hear a train approaching.

168. Question: What should you do when you see a "Pedestrian Crossing" sign?
Answer: Be alert for pedestrians and yield the right-of-way when necessary.

169. Question: What should you do when you see a "Yield to Bicycles" sign?

Answer: Yield the right-of-way to bicycles when necessary.

170. Question: What should you do when you encounter a "Bicycle Lane" sign?
Answer: Be aware that you are entering a bicycle lane; do not drive in it.

171. Question: What should you do when you see a "Share the Road" sign with a bicycle symbol?
Answer: Be aware that you should share the road with bicycles.

172. Question: What should you do when you encounter a "Watch for Bicyclists" sign?
Answer: Be alert for bicycles on the road.

173. Question: What should you do when you see a "Watch for Children" sign?
Answer: Be cautious and drive slowly, especially in areas with children.

174. Question: What should you do when you encounter a "Watch for Animals" sign?
Answer: Be cautious and watch for animals, especially in rural areas.

175. Question: What should you do when you see a "Slippery When Wet" sign?
Answer: Slow down and be cautious, especially in wet conditions.

176. Question: What should you do when you see a "Reduced Speed Limit" sign?
Answer: Obey the posted speed limit indicated on the sign.

177. Question: What should you do when you see a "Construction Zone" sign?
Answer: Be prepared to slow down, follow detours, and be cautious in construction areas.

178. Question: What should you do when you see a "Road Work Ahead" sign?
Answer: Be prepared for road work and slow down.

179. Question: What should you do when you encounter a "Merge" sign?
Answer: Prepare to merge with traffic from another lane.

180. Question: What should you do when you see a "Lane Ends" sign?
Answer: Be prepared for the lane to end, and merge into the available lane.

181. Question: What should you do when you see a "No Passing" sign?

Answer: Do not pass other vehicles in the area indicated by the sign.

182. Question: What should you do when you encounter a "Two-Way Traffic" sign?

Answer: Be aware that you are entering a two-way traffic zone.

183. Question: What should you do when you see a "Do Not Enter" sign on a one-way street?

Answer: Do not enter the street in the wrong direction.

184. Question: What should you do when you see a "Wrong Way" sign on a freeway off-ramp?

Answer: Do not enter the off-ramp in the wrong direction.

185. Question: What should you do when you see a "Do Not Pass" sign?

Answer: Do not pass other vehicles in the area indicated by the sign.

186. Question: What should you do when you encounter a "No Trucks" sign?

Answer: Do not enter the road if you are driving a truck.

187. Question: What should you do when you see a "Stop" sign?
Answer: Come to a complete stop and yield the right-of-way.

188. Question: What should you do when you see a "One Lane Bridge" sign?
Answer: Yield the right-of-way to oncoming traffic when crossing the bridge.

189. Question: What should you do when you encounter a "Road Narrows" sign?
Answer: Be prepared for a narrower roadway ahead.

190. Question: What should you do when you see a "Winding Road" sign?
Answer: Be prepared for a road with many curves or turns.

191. Question: What should you do when you see a "Cross Road" sign?
Answer: Be prepared for an intersection where another road crosses the one you are on.

192. Question: What should you do when you see a "Stop Ahead" sign?

Answer: Be prepared to come to a complete stop ahead.

193. Question: What should you do when you see a "Yield Ahead" sign?
Answer: Be prepared to yield the right-of-way ahead.

194. Question: What should you do when you see a "Signal Ahead" sign?
Answer: Be prepared for a traffic signal ahead.

195. Question: What should you do when you see a "Curve Ahead" sign?
Answer: Be prepared for a curve or turn in the road ahead.

196. Question: What should you do when you see a "Deer Crossing" sign?
Answer: Be cautious and watch for deer crossing the road, especially in rural areas.

197. Question: What should you do when you see a "No Outlet" sign?
Answer: Be prepared for a dead-end road or a road with no exit.

198. Question: What should you do when you see a "Watch for Falling Rocks" sign?

Answer: Be cautious and watch for rocks or debris in the road, especially in mountainous areas.

199. Question: What should you do when you see a "Pavement Ends" sign?
Answer: Be prepared for the road to change from paved to unpaved.

200. Question: What should you do when you see a "Bicycle Crossing" sign?
Answer: Be cautious and watch for bicycles crossing the road.

201. Question: What should you do when you see a "Horse Crossing" sign?
Answer: Be cautious and watch for horses crossing the road.

202. Question: What should you do when you see a "Low Clearance" sign?
Answer: Be cautious and watch for low clearance structures, such as bridges or tunnels.

203. Question: What should you do when you see a "No Turn on Red" sign after a turn lane?
Answer: Do not make a right turn on a red traffic signal when indicated by the sign.

204. Question: What should you do when you see a "School Zone" sign?
Answer: Slow down and be cautious, especially when children are present.

205. Question: What should you do when you see a "Pedestrian Crossing" sign with a speed limit on it?
Answer: Obey the posted speed limit and be cautious for pedestrians.

206. Question: What should you do when you see a "Speed Limit" sign?
Answer: Obey the posted speed limit indicated by the sign.

207. Question: What should you do when you see a "No Right Turn on Red" sign?
Answer: Do not make a right turn on a red traffic signal at that location.

208. Question: What should you do when you see a "No Left Turn on Red" sign?
Answer: Do not make a left turn on a red traffic signal at that location.

209. Question: What should you do when you see a "No U-Turn" sign at an intersection?

Answer: Do not make a U-turn at that location.

210. Question: What should you do when you see a "Keep Right" sign with a left arrow?
Answer: Stay to the right and follow the direction indicated by the sign.

211. Question: What should you do when you see a "Keep Left" sign with a right arrow?
Answer: Stay to the left and follow the direction indicated by the sign.

212. Question: What should you do when you see a "Do Not Pass" sign with a dashed line?
Answer: Do not pass other vehicles in the area indicated by the sign.

213. Question: What should you do when you see a "Divided Highway Begins" sign?
Answer: Be prepared for a divided highway ahead with a median or barrier.

214. Question: What should you do when you see a "Divided Highway Ends" sign?
Answer: Be prepared for the end of a divided highway with a median or barrier.

215. Question: What should you do when you see a "No Bicycles" sign?

Answer: Do not allow bicycles on the road where the sign is posted.

216. Question: What should you do when you see a "No Pedestrians" sign?

Answer: Do not allow pedestrians on the road where the sign is posted.

217. Question: What should you do when you see a "One Way" sign pointing in the opposite direction?

Answer: You are going the wrong way; turn around and go in the direction indicated by the sign.

218. Question: What should you do when you see a "Do Not Enter" sign on an exit ramp?

Answer: Do not enter the exit ramp; you are going the wrong way.

219. Question: What should you do when you see a "Reduced Speed Limit Ahead" sign?

Answer: Be prepared to obey a reduced speed limit ahead.

220. Question: What should you do when you see a "Roundabout" sign?

Answer: Be prepared to enter a roundabout.

Printed in Great Britain
by Amazon

46303265R00036